**DATE DUE**

36932

## STOCKTON
## Township Public Library
### Stockton, IL

# BUTTERNUT HOLLOW POND

BY BRIAN J. HEINZ

ILLUSTRATED BY BOB MARSTALL

The Millbrook Press – Brookfield, Connecticut

Published by The Millbrook Press, Inc.
2 Old New Milford Road
Brookfield, Connecticut 06804

Book design by Tania Garcia

Library of Congress Cataloging-in-Publication Data

Heinz, Brian J., 1946-
  Butternut Hollow Pond / Brian J. Heinz ; illustrated by Bob Marstall.
      p. cm.
  Summary: Five vignettes, from dawn to midnight, present the dramat-
ic dynamics of survival and competition in and around a typical
North American pond, featuring such animals as a pickerel frog,
water snake, and opossum.
  ISBN 0-7613-0268-9 (lib.) – ISBN 0-7613-1325-7 (trade)
    1. Pond animals—Juvenile literature. 2. Predation (Biology)—
Juvenile literature. [1. Pond animals. 2. Pond ecology. 3. Ecology.] I.
Marstall, Bob, ill.  II. Title

QL146.3 . H45 2000
591.763—dc21
        99-044813

library ed.  5  4  3  2  1
trade ed.  5  4  3  2  1

For my nieces, Ashley and Nicole.   —B.J.H.

For Sister Gabriel Mary Hoare, S.L., a wonderful mentor and
teacher whose patience, grace, trust, and wisdom helped me
through college— and inspires me still.   —B.M.

# Daybreak at Butternut Hollow Pond

Sunbeams fall in slender shafts through a canopy of swamp maples. The water is dappled in a confetti of pale light. Dewdrops sparkle on the reeds.

A warm breeze ripples over the water and awakens the insects along the shore. Water striders stand on delicate legs, skating the surface in short pulses. Below them, whirligig beetles tumble and dive in the shallows like a troupe of acrobats. It is not safe here.

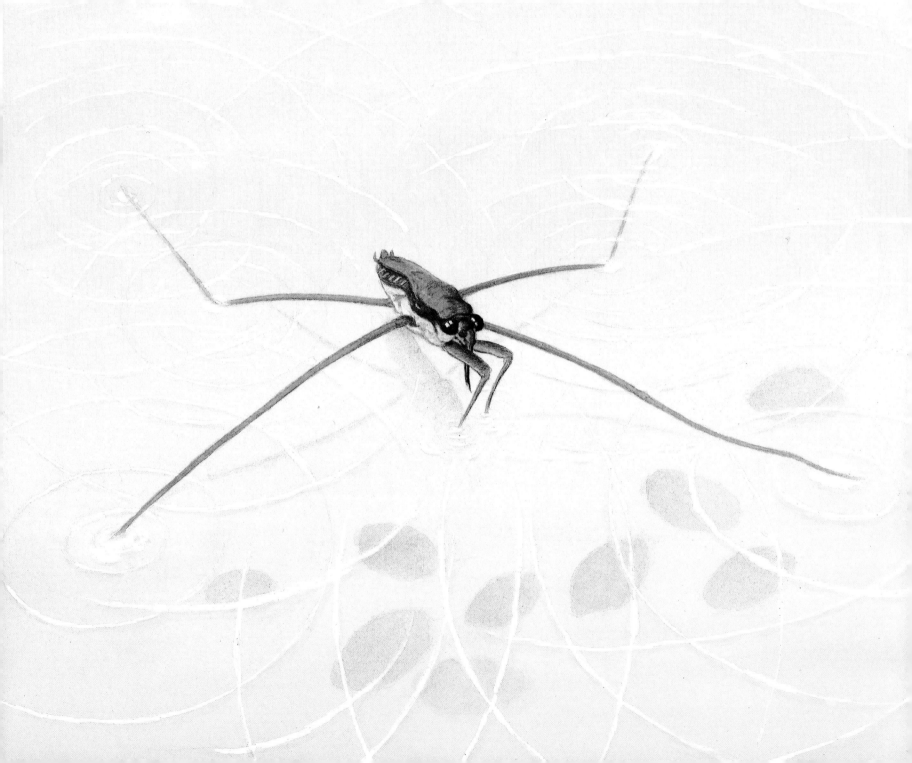

Young bluegills hover under a blanket of duckweed and dart out to gobble up the unlucky insects.

Mosquitoes, gnats, and mayflies rise from shore grasses on lacy wings. A breath of air carries them over the water. There is danger here, too.

A dragonfly cruises in at high speed, his doubled wings beating a blur above his gleaming green body. Snap! Snap! Mosquitoes are snatched in midair by his powerful jaws. But even the dragonfly is not safe.

The tree swallows are here, too. *Swoosh!* The birds plummet from the branches, looping and diving like combat aircraft. Their sharp wings tilt and twist in sudden turns as they pursue their prey. Their short beaks open wide and the insects disappear. A moment later the dragonfly is gone. It's good to be quick in Butternut Hollow.

# MIDMORNING AT BUTTERNUT HOLLOW POND

F ive mallard ducklings take to the water, weaving behind their parents like floats in a parade. They tip their fuzzy bottoms up and pull away soft mouthfuls of water shamrock.

But deep in the mud a monster lies in wait. He has heard the splashing. He has seen the tiny webbed feet kicking above him. And he rises slowly.

The snapping turtle drags his heavy body from the pond bottom. Long strands of green algae cover the jagged shell on his back. He stretches his long neck upward and opens his powerful beak.

*Splash! Crack!* The gaping jaws slam shut as the water boils around him.

*Quack! Quack!* Flapping madly, the ducks charge for cover under an overhang of roots at the pond's bank. Mother and Father mallard count their brood. One. Two. Three. Four. Five.

Sometimes you're lucky in Butternut Hollow.

A few downy feathers bob on the ripples as the great turtle sinks out of sight and settles in the dark ooze to wait again.

The commotion has disturbed a pumpkinseed, which bursts from the shadows seeking safety. He has made a mistake. Another hunter is waiting as the speckled sides of the fish flash briefly in the sunlight.

The heron has been patient, motionless. Quick as a blink, the long bill stabs the water. The fish is seized and swallowed whole. And the heron is still again.

# Noon at Butternut Hollow Pond

❧

On the hillside meadow above the pond, wildflowers sway in a crazy quilt of colors. The air is filled with the songs of a hundred bees.

A woodchuck trims the sweet grasses as his rumbly body shuffles aimlessly over the ground. Nearby, a cottontail suddenly sits erect. He listens. He looks. A broad shadow passes over the hill.

The cottontail explodes into motion and zigzags into the blackberry thickets. Now the woodchuck knows. Something is not right in Butternut Hollow and he scrambles for his burrow.

The marsh hawk ends his swift glide, trapping the air in splayed feathers. The woodchuck clambers along just ahead. The hawk's curved talons stretch out before him, but they close on nothing as the woodchuck disappears into his hole.

The hawk turns and beats his way upward until he is once again scouting Butternut Hollow in wide circles, while a white-tailed deer leads her fawn to drink at the cool water.

# End of day at Butternut Hollow Pond

The sky is blushed and, for a moment, all is still.
A pickerel frog clings to a gnarled branch poking above the water.
His head lowers slightly as his round eyes watch a moth flutter to rest
on the branch. The frog takes aim. His sticky tongue flies out and …
*slurp!* The moth is taken.

The frog pushes his way up the branch and suddenly freezes. He does not blink. He does not breathe. He does not dare. Again, the hunter has become the hunted.

A water snake curls along slowly, his head above the water, passing just under the branch. The snake is a skillful and silent swimmer, scarcely disturbing the surface.

The pickerel frog waits long minutes then leaps into the water, thrusting toward shelter in the tall reeds on his broad webbed feet. But sometimes there is just no escape in Butternut Hollow.

A largemouth bass bursts upward from a tangle of leathery roots, and the frog vanishes into the fish's gaping maw. Everyone is hungry at Butternut Hollow Pond.

As the bass circles back, *kerploosh!* Something hits the water above him. Dangling legs seem to struggle and twitch. The bass strikes at another meal. But not this time. The object is hard. It pulls violently at the fish's jaw and is dragged forward. Moments later, a young boy hauls him in on rod and reel. The hunters come in many forms at Butternut Hollow.

# Night at Butternut Hollow Pond

❧

The water shimmers under moonglow, and wisps of fog dance over the pond like ghosts. It is not quiet. There is a raucous concert of frogs and toads and crickets and katydids, croaking and chirping from dark hideaways.

The night is a free-for-all at Butternut Hollow Pond.

Small brown bats dash and dip over the water, snapping up one bug after another. Above the treetops, the nighthawks are at work too.

Crayfish creep up the banks searching for night crawlers that have wriggled up from the spongy soil. Raccoons prowl along the shore grabbing the crayfish from the damp grass.

Mother opossum is here, too. Her babies cling to the fur on her back as she crunches down on a tiger beetle.

The blacksnake slithers unseen, flicking his dainty tongue, watching for a twitch of movement. Somewhere, there is a toad. Somewhere.

There are voles and moles, a fox and a screech owl. All are part of the night shift in Butternut Hollow.

A kingfisher roosts for the night and awaits the next dawn at Butternut Hollow Pond, where the hunters and the hunted are one and the same, and tomorrow is just another day.